PROFESSIONALIZATION, LEADERSHIP AND MANAGEMENT IN THE EARLY YEARS

The Critical Issues in the Early Years Series

This series provides both national (UK wide) and international perspectives on critical issues within the field of early years education and care.

The quality of early childhood education and care (ECEC) has remained a high priority on government agendas in recent years (OECD, 2006). This series reflects this developing early childhood context which includes professionalizing, and up-skilling, the early childhood workforce. In particular, the series brings a critical perspective to the developing knowledge and understanding of early years practitioners at various stages of their professional development, to encourage reflection on practice and to bring to their attention key themes and issues in the field of early childhood.

Series Editor

Linda Miller is Professor Emeritus of Early Years at The Open University. Since 2005 Linda has been co-director of international project 'Day in the Life of an Early Years Practitioner' based within the European Early Childhood Research Association (EECERA). She is currently on the Expert Advisory Group for an EU study on Competencies in Early Childhood Education (ECE) and is co-lead researcher for the England case study. She has been a member of government stakeholder groups and working parties concerned with workforce development in the early years. Linda has written and co-edited a wide range of books for early years practitioners, and has published in national and international journals.

Reference

Organisation for Economic Co-operation and Development (OECD) (2006) *Starting Strong II: Early Childhood Education and Care.* Paris: OECD.

Titles in the series

Miller and Cable, *Professionalization, Leadership and Management in the Early Years*
Miller and Heavey, *Policy Issues in the Early Years*
Miller and Pound, *Theories and Approaches to Learning in the Early Years*

PROFESSIONALIZATION, LEADERSHIP AND MANAGEMENT IN THE EARLY YEARS

Edited by
Linda Miller and Carrie Cable

Los Angeles | London | New Delhi
Singapore | Washington DC

Editorial arrangement, Chapter 1 and Chapter 11
© Linda Miller and Carrie Cable 2011
Chapter 2 © Mary E. Whalley 2011
Chapter 3 © Christine Woodrow 2011
Chapter 4 © Dorothy McMillan and Glenda Walsh 2011
Chapter 5 © Jan Peeters and Michel Vandenbroeck 2011
Chapter 6 © Sue Greenfield 2011
Chapter 7 © Gill McGillivray 2011
Chapter 8 © Jayne Osgood 2011
Chapter 9 © Guy Roberts-Holmes and Simon Brownhill 2011
Chapter 10 © Iris Duhn 2011

First published 2011

SAGE Publications Ltd
1 Oliver's Yard
55 City Road
London EC1Y 1SP

SAGE Publications Inc.
2455 Teller Road
Thousand Oaks, California 91320

SAGE Publications India Pvt Ltd
B 1/I 1 Mohan Cooperative Industrial Area
Mathura Road
New Delhi 110 044

SAGE Publications Asia-Pacific Pte Ltd
33 Pekin Street #02-01
Far East Square
Singapore 048763

Library of Congress Control Number: 2010926071

British Library Cataloguing in Publication data

A catalogue record for this book is available from the British Library

ISBN 978-1-84920-553-5
ISBN 978-1-84920-554-2 (pbk)

Typeset by C&M Digitals (P) Ltd, Chennai, India
Printed and bound in Great Britain by TJ International Ltd, Padstow, Cornwall
Printed on paper from sustainable resources

Mixed Sources
Product group from well-managed
forests and other controlled sources
www.fsc.org Cert no. SGS-COC-2482
FSC © 1996 Forest Stewardship Council

Education at SAGE

SAGE is a leading international publisher of journals, books, and electronic media for academic, educational, and professional markets.

Our education publishing includes:

- accessible and comprehensive texts for aspiring education professionals and practitioners looking to further their careers through continuing professional development

- inspirational advice and guidance for the classroom

- authoritative state of the art reference from the leading authors in the field

Find out more at: **www.sagepub.co.uk/education**

CONTENTS

ABOUT THE EDITORS AND CONTRIBUTORS

Editors

Linda Miller is Professor Emeritus of Early Years at The Open University. Since 2005 Linda has been co-director of international project 'Day in the Life of an Early Years Practitioner' based within the European Early Childhood Research Association (EECERA). She is currently on the Expert Advisory Group for an EU study on Competencies in Early Childhood Education (ECE) and is co-lead researcher for the England case study. She has been a member of government stakeholder groups and working parties concerned with workforce development in the early years. Linda has written and co-edited a wide range of books for early years practitioners, and has published in national and international journals.

Carrie Cable is a Senior Lecturer in Education at The Open University and was Director of a major Department for Children, Schools and Families (now Department for Education) (DCSF)-funded longitudinal research project examining the learning and teaching of languages in primary schools from 2007 to 2010. Carrie has been involved in teaching and research relating to primary and early years education for many years. Other research interests include English as an Additional Language (EAL) and bilingualism. She co-edited *Professionalism in the Early Years*, with Linda Miller (2008) (Hodder Education).

Contributors

Simon Brownhill is a Senior Lecturer in the Education Studies Department at the University of Derby and has taught on a range of early years and primary programmes, including the Foundation Degree, Bachelor of Education and Masters in Education.

He was formerly Assistant Headteacher of Early Years in a large, culturally diverse, inner-city primary school. Simon continues to actively work with children aged 3–13 in a variety of educational settings. His teaching and research interests include developing creativity in the classroom, supporting learners from culturally diverse backgrounds and the ambiguities of the male role model in the early years (0–8). He has written a number of single and co-authored books on effective behaviour management, and writes for the parenting magazine *Junior*.

Iris Duhn lectures in the School of Critical Studies in Education, Faculty of Education, the University of Auckland. Her teaching and research focuses on globalization, ecological sustainability, and governmentality studies. Her publications and research projects contribute a critical childhood studies perspective to early childhood education in New Zealand, and internationally.

Sue Greenfield is a Senior Lecturer in Early Childhood Studies at Roehampton University. She originally trained as a health visitor, working with children and families, and later was head of a 60-place nursery. Her research interests are in working in partnership, both with parents and in multidisciplinary teams. She is particularly interested in the concept of partnership and ways in which partnerships evolve.

Gill McGillivray is Senior Lecturer in Early Childhood Education and Care at Newman University College in Birmingham. Previous posts have included teaching in further education on Early Years Care and Education and Psychology programmes. Current research interests include the construction of professional identities in the early years workforce in England. She is also leading a funded international project with partners in Romania and Poland on 'Play and Learning in the Early Years for Inclusion'.

Dorothy McMillan is a Senior Lecturer in Early Childhood Education at Stranmillis University College, Belfast, where she teaches on the BEd, PGCE (Early Years), BA and MA in Early Childhood Studies degree programmes. Her doctoral thesis focused on the conceptual notion of 'educare' in preschool settings and its implications for early years training. Her current research interests are focused on training, qualifications and early years professionalism, management and leadership and parental partnerships.

Jayne Osgood is a Reader at London Metropolitan University. She has a background in critical feminist approaches to early childhood education and has research interests in critical discourse analysis, autobiographical narrative methods and theorizing identity construction, and has published widely on these issues. Her forthcoming book *Narratives from the Nursery* is due for publication in late 2010.

Jan Peeters is co-ordinator of VBJK, Research and Resource Centre for Early Childhood Education and Care (University of Ghent). He has directed several

European projects on professionalism in ECEC. He is a co-founder of the European Diversity in Early Childhood Education and Training (DECET) network on diversity and training in ECEC. He is the author of a book on professionalism in ECEC in New Zealand, France, England and Denmark: *The Construction of a New Profession*. He co-founded the European magazine *Children in Europe* and was guest editor of an issue on professionalism: 'Aiming high: a professional workforce for the early years'. He worked as consultant for the International Step by Step Association. Together with Professor Vandenbroeck and Professor Mathias Urban, he is director of the EU study on Competencies in ECE.

Guy Roberts-Holmes is a Senior Lecturer in Early Years Education in the Department of Early Childhood and Primary Education at the Institute of Education, University of London. He is the Programme Leader for the Masters in Early Years Education. His teaching and research focus is on the professional development of the early childhood workforce, early childhood pedagogy, inclusion and diversity, men and fathers in early childhood services, and early childhood research methodology. His funded research projects include an evaluation of the quality impact of Early Years Professionals (EYPs) in early years settings and an investigation of practitioners' experiences of the Early Years Foundation Stage (EYFS) in England.

Michel Vandenbroeck is Professor in Family Pedagogy and Early Childhood Care and Education at the Department of Social Welfare Studies of Ghent University, Belgium. His main research interests are in childcare, parent support and issues of diversity and social inclusion. He has authored several books and international publications on these issues. He is a member of the editorial board of the *European Early Childhood Education Research Journal* and is president of the board of the VBJK (www.vbjk.be) Research and Resource Centre on Early Childhood Education in Flanders (Belgium). Together with Dr Jan Peeters, he co-founded the European network Diversity in Early Childhood Education and Training (www.decet.org). Currently he co-chairs a global Learning Group on Program Development in Contexts of Ethnic Segregation, as a part of the global learning initiative Una (www.una.org).

Glenda Walsh is a Principal Lecturer in Early Childhood Education at Stranmillis University College, Belfast where she teaches on a range of early years programmes and is course director of the Post Graduate Certificate in Early Years. Her research interests fall into the field of quality issues and early years pedagogy. Her doctoral thesis concentrated on the play versus formal education debate in Northern Ireland and Denmark. The observation instrument she devised has been used as the main assessment instrument in the Early Years Enriched Curriculum Evaluation Project in Northern Ireland.

Mary E. Whalley is a tutor on the Foundation Degree 'Young Children's Learning and Development' and BA Hons in Childhood Studies at Leeds Metropolitan University and Harrogate College. She also works as an independent consultant in early years practice. She has had close involvement in the development of the early years workforce including leading a government-sponsored project to consider work-based learning. Mary also works as a tutor and assessor of Early Years Professional Status with Best Practice Network. Her research interests include the leadership aspect of the Early Years Professional role and Children's Workforce development in England.

Christine Woodrow is Associate Professor and a researcher and teacher educator specializing in early years education at the University of Western Sydney. In addition to being a passionate advocate for early childhood educators, and their role as leaders of change, Christine researches in the areas of early childhood policy, curriculum and professional identity. She is project leader of an innovative early childhood community project, 'Futuro Infantil Hoy', which is exploring innovative pedagogical practice through communities of practice in early childhood contexts in northern Chile.

ACKNOWLEDGEMENTS

Iris Duhn, the author of Chapter 10, would like to thank the teaching team at Collectively Kids, in particular Marina, Kate, Julia and Vanessa for their co-theorization of data, and the New Zealand Teaching and Learning Research Initiative (TLRI) for research funding, with a special thank you to Maliah for her insights.

CHAPTER 1

THE CHANGING FACE OF PROFESSIONALISM IN THE EARLY YEARS

Linda Miller and Carrie Cable

Overview

This book has given space to a group of academics, trainers of early years practitioners and researchers to present a collection of individual perspectives on professionalism, leadership and management in the early years. Many of the chapters in the book present demanding and stimulating ideas and views on the professionalization of the early years workforce which we hope will challenge and unsettle you and encourage you to engage in a dialogue about the nature of professionalism, as Dalli and Urban envisage '... *professionalism* can be understood as a *discourse* as much as a phenomenon: as something that is constantly under reconstruction' (Dalli and Urban, 2008: 132).

We hope the book will help you to reflect upon your current thinking and practice and your developing professionalism in new and critical ways. A number of chapters openly contest policy reforms and public discourses in particular geographical and cultural contexts and as Osgood (2006) says, the cost of *not* doing this is just too high. In this introductory chapter, we offer an overview of the growth of professionalism in the early years over the last decade and identify some key emerging themes, many of which are raised in the ensuing chapters.

(Continued)

(Continued)

In this chapter, we outline the structure of the book and its rationale. Throughout the book, the terms early years and early childhood education and care are used interchangeably to reflect the international contributions. 'Early years' is a term more commonly used in the United Kingdom (UK) to reflect the bringing together of both care and education under one policy umbrella. Early years education and care is generally used in Europe and beyond and reflects the historical and separate development of early childhood services under a two-tier organization of services emphasizing childcare for the youngest children (up to age 3) and 'pre-primary education' for the 3–6 year olds (OECD, 2006). In this book, we take the view that the early years/early childhood field should be seen as 'educational' but with a care component and that it should be impossible to educate without caring, or care without developing and promoting children's learning. We also use the term 'she' when referring to individuals of both genders, which seems appropriate in a book which is about a heavily feminized workforce.

The growth of professionalism in the early years

As this book shows, the professionalization of those who work, lead and manage in early years settings has been on an upward trajectory for at least the last decade, both nationally and internationally. The growth of early years professionalism has had different starting points and has followed different paths within the countries covered in the chapters in this book. Individuals are also on a continuum of professional development and will vary at any point in time in relation to their professional knowledge, understanding and skills. The range and variety of spaces they are working in, the cultural, geographical and policy context of their work, working relationships and pedagogic practices will define, limit or expand opportunities for the development of their professionalism.

A recent Google search of 'professionalism in the early years' gave rise to 1,780,000 hits – reflecting the raft of initiatives, books, journal articles and policy documents published in the last decade or so, both in the UK and internationally. We begin by looking back at some selected publications which also document this growth.

In 1998, Abbott and Pugh's book *Training to Work in the Early Years* brought together both developments and concerns about early years training in the UK and internationally and documented some of the then new routes to training such as Early Childhood Studies Degrees and National Vocational Qualifications. A chapter by Oberheumer (1998) detailed the European perspective. In the final chapter, a 'climbing frame of qualifications' was envisaged (p. 149) offering a training route to higher levels of qualifications and increased access to professional development for the early years workforce.

In 2003, as part of a literature review of aspects of predominantly British-based and recent early years research, members of the British Educational Research Association Special Interest Group, including one of the editors of this book (Linda Miller), undertook responsibility for reviewing a selection of the literature on adult roles, training and professionalism. This part of the review concluded that:

- there was no national database identifying the nature of early years settings
- there was a plethora of occupational names that were not useful in identifying workplace roles
- the Qualifications and Curriculum Authority was attempting to classify occupational roles
- a series of surveys organized by the Early Years National Training Organisation was beginning to compile information on occupational roles
- there was a paucity of evidence about links between adult training, professionalism and children's learning.

A decade on, Miller and Cable (2008) sought to update the position of early years workers and document the tremendous policy changes and 'workforce reform' that had taken place and the opportunities for achieving professional qualifications, both in the UK and internationally. The title of the book *Professionalism in the Early Years* reflects the conceptual shift that has taken place since the publication of Abbott and Pugh's book a decade before and also mirrors government policies on 'reforming' and professionalizing the early years workforce in England and in other countries. However, alongside this reform process critical voices were emerging (Miller, 2008). Critics of the reform process challenged those involved in the teaching and training of early years workers to rethink this emerging construction of professionalism which they saw as being constrained by technological practices (Dahlberg and Moss, 2005) and underpinned by the 'regulatory gaze' of government (Osgood, 2006: 3). However, more recently Simpson (2010: 12) has added to the debate, using data from a study of Early Years Professionals (EYPs) in England, arguing that they have a 'bounded agency' and a 'reflexive professionalism' which is 'mediated by reflexivity over circumstances that were potentially enabling or restrictive'.

This movement towards professionalism and the accompanying critiques forms the basis for the notion of 'a critical ecology of the profession' (Dalli, 2007, unpaged). The use of the term 'ecology' relates to the type of contexts or environments within which a practitioner works and the influence of micro and macro level factors, which in turn create possibilities for the types of practice that can take place. According to Dalli, the use of the term 'a critical ecology of the profession' is intended to suggest that a questioning approach to how professionals might act in these different geographical, physical and cultural contexts is critical in developing our understanding. In other words, the early childhood community needs to stand back and adopt a critical approach to all constructions of professionalism and consider context-specific factors.

Since 2004, a group of academics, researchers and trainers of practitioners (including the editors of this book) located within the European Early Childhood Education Research Association (EECERA) have, through research project 'A Day in the Life of an Early Years Practitioner' (Miller et al., forthcoming), sought to explore what it means to act professionally in different contexts. Researchers worked with an individual practitioner, each working in an early childhood setting in one of six countries (Australia, England, Finland, Germany, New Zealand and Sweden) to explore practitioner notions of professionalism. This included:

- perceptions of what being a 'professional' in early childhood means – including practitioners' self perceptions and external perspectives
- common features of practice in each context.

The 'Day in the Life' project is a collection of free-standing but related case studies and does not and cannot provide comparative data across countries and cultures. However, some common themes have been identified, including the complexity and diversity of working professionally with young children and the ways in which government agendas set the context for 'feeling and acting professionally'. These themes and others are expanded upon in the chapters in this book.

In England, the development of professionalism has been confused and confounded by the creation of a new role which includes professional in its title – the Early Years Professional (see Chapters 2 and 7) – which raises questions about whether those who do *not* have this title or another accepted title such as 'teacher' are therefore deemed not to be 'professionals'. Moss (2008) takes up the argument about this contradictory position, supporting the vision of a professional workforce but one which recognizes core workers as professionals as well as leaders. Writing in an Australian context, Fenech and Sumsion (2007: 119) also urge a note of caution in relation to the professionalization of the workforce and warn of the 'othering' of less qualified or non-accredited practitioners.

On a related theme, Oberheumer and Scheryer (2008) have documented and mapped some of the current changes taking place across 27 European countries in the professionalization strategies for work in early childhood provision, including qualification profiles across and within these countries. Issues raised by this study include whether traditional demarcation lines between early childhood workers will remain; for example, between the role of the primary school teacher and the early years pedagogues. Oberheumer's and Scheryer's research reveals no agreement across Europe on the competence requirements for working with young children up to the age of school entry and therefore no common understanding of what 'professionalism' in the early years means. The researchers raise questions about whether there will be a common consensus about the type of professional we want in early childhood work – a 'democratic professional' that values reciprocal relationships and alliances and places children, families and communities at the centre of their work or a 'technical expert' focused on prescribed routes and outcomes.

The chapters in this book contribute and add to this growing debate. In Part 1, the chapters are concerned mainly with the professional identities of early years practitioners and in Part 2, they look towards a new professionalism.

Part 1: Leading, managing and new professional identities

The chapters in this section are concerned with the developing professional identities of early years practitioners, whether as the core workers envisaged by Peter Moss (2008) or as leaders and managers in early years settings.

In Chapter 2, Mary Whalley notes that *leadership* and *management* are terms often used interchangeably which she sees as unhelpful. In the chapter, she clarifies the different emphases of the two roles of leader and manager as change agents in relation to early years provision and explores the distinctive and distinguishing features of these key roles. She considers the Early Years Professional role in England in leading practice and the challenges facing those professionals leading organizations such as Integrated Children's Centres, which require working in a multi-professional context. She also considers the contribution of research, theory and influences from Europe and beyond to a new understanding of professionalism.

Christine Woodrow in Chapter 3 tracks some emerging and worrying policy trends in early childhood provision in Australia and considers their impact on discourses of professionalism and on early childhood practitioners. Through three 'cases' of recent policy directions or policy outcome, she analyses and discusses the implications for professional identity. She raises concerns about the significant growth in market-led provision, increased regulation and accountability and contradictions within the Australian early childhood reform agenda. She describes the impact this is having on the professional identities of the early childhood workforce, their practices and their relationships with children and parents. Woodrow points to disturbing parallels with England where she contends simplistic solutions have been sought to achieve complex outcomes and where short-term policies have sought to bring about rapid growth and change, both in terms of increased provision and in expanding and 'professionalizing' the workforce. The collapse of a large corporate childcare company in Australia sounds warning bells about the privatization of early childhood provision as a means of achieving substantial growth. Whilst welcoming increased political interest in early childhood provision, Woodrow questions how dominant policy discourses might constrain, affirm or expand understandings of professionalism and perspectives on professional identity. She argues for multiple professional identities and discusses the notion of 'networked leadership' and the need to resource new leadership roles to sustain this changing agenda.

Chapter 4 considers early years policy and provision in Northern Ireland, where despite policy initiatives which reflect the strategy in England, early childhood services are provided through a 'split system' of care and education which continues to differentiate between the traditional childcare and education sectors. Dorothy McMillan and Glenda Walsh explore the notion of early years professionalism within such a context and pose the question, 'What is to be done?' They note that it is necessary to chart both the 'historical baggage' and recent developments in order to consider some current issues around the 'new era' of early years professionalism in Northern Ireland. These include issues around power and agency and the need to challenge dominant discourses. They consider future possibilities for the Northern Ireland workforce in terms of lead roles and qualifications across the sector, including the possibility of a new early years sector with a sense of a collective professional identity.

Jan Peeters and Michel Vandenbroeck, based in the University of Ghent, document their work with early childhood workers over three decades. In Chapter 5, they chart the professional journeys of these practitioners through testimonies which show how, through engaging with pedagogic guidance, they became 'actors of change' and developed new pedagogic practices. Peeters and Vandenbroeck stress the importance of higher-level qualifications in order to achieve quality provision in early childhood settings, but just as important, they stress, is the need to create space for reflection and reflexivity. By providing such a space and support for the practitioners in their study, these practitioners were able to actively engage, collaborate and construct their professionalism and new professional identities. As the authors contend, the most significant evolutions occurred when representatives of the sector, academia and policy-makers collaborated in democratic ways to develop new types of professionalism. This more localized approach to the professionalization of the workforce offers an alternative to national and highly regulated frameworks for professional development in countries such as England.

Multi-professional working is seen by governments as a solution to the complex problems facing those working with children, young people and their families and refers to both co-operation with professionals from other sectors and 'multi-professional operations' within settings (Karila, 2008: 214). The chapter by Sue Greenfield explores some of the challenges that occur around the notion of professional identities when professionals from different backgrounds are asked to work together and cross professional boundaries. She explores why multidisciplinary working can be problematic and difficult to accomplish and considers the barriers to successful working practices. The chapter considers issues such as professional 'cultures', language, lead roles and key responsibilities. Whilst policy initiatives commit professionals to the ideal of integrated working, in order to improve outcomes for children and young people, the reality can be different. The chapter looks at the background to the move towards integrated working and measures that have been taken to promote this. Consideration is given as to whether this way of working is possible and why it is so desirable.

Part 2: Towards a new professionalism in the early years

In the quote in the chapter overview, Dalli and Urban (2008) suggest that a conceptualization of professionalism in the early years should be viewed as an ongoing process rather than as a 'once and for all' phenomenon. We have seen from the introduction to the chapters in Part 1 of this book that constructions of professionalism are in the process of being transformed and that early years practitioners are key to this process as 'actors of change' working within learning communities or 'communities of practice' (Wenger, 1998). Karila (2008) talks about professionalism as a 'multi level phenomenon' influenced by macro level changes (for example, government policy and priorities) and micro level changes (the everyday working environment and the culture of the workplace), all of which raises questions and expectations about professionalism in the field of early childhood. The chapters in this section look to the future and reflect the growth of new ways of looking at and thinking about professionalism.

In Chapter 7, Gill McGillivray considers the many complex influences that help to construct and shape the professional identities of practitioners within the early years workforce, particularly in England. She explores both micro and macro level influences, including the working context and culture and the dominant discourses to which practitioners are exposed. She sees personal life histories of practitioners as an important factor, arguing that the sense of who we are cannot be dissociated from our professional identities. In offering a profile of the workforce, she acknowledges the inequalities that exist and the need for opportunities for better qualifications, but cautions that this may suggest a message of 'not good enough' to core workers who may not have a level 3 qualification and even to those who do. She ends the chapter with suggestions for looking forward to a time when working with young children is recognized as a worthwhile career.

In the next chapter, Jayne Osgood develops an argument for 'professionalism from within'. Like Gill McGillivray, she notes the significance of autobiography and the subjective experiences of day-to-day working practices of practitioners as important for conceptualizing professionalism differently. She draws on a study of nursery staff from the private, voluntary and statutory sectors, who whilst reluctantly accepting the dominance of government discourses in discussions about what it means to be professional, did not include, for example, dominant notions of accountability, measurability and the need to demonstrate measurable outcomes. She argues that their professionalism was shaped by a commitment to 'an ethics of care and critical reflection' and for the promotion of the 'critically reflective emotional professional' in place of the 'competent technician'.

Chapter 9 asks 'Where are the men?' in early years work. Guy Roberts-Holmes and Simon Brownhill question why the early years workforce remains predominantly female, both nationally, and to a slightly lesser extent, internationally, given current cultural and economic shifts to address this issue. They examine the historical construction of early years work as traditionally and naturally feminine, which they argue, coupled with fears of masculine sexuality, helps to explain the maintenance of this position. They argue this position is compounded by a working culture or 'vocational habitus' which is inclusive of stereotypical feminine traits but excludes those traits deemed 'masculine'. This also includes factors such as traditionally low pay and low status and the increasing privatization and marketization of early years provision. Through case studies, they highlight the struggles of men working in the early years and examine UK-based and international projects and initiatives that have successfully included men as early years practitioners. They conclude that it is the pedagogical and interpersonal skills of the practitioner and not gender that is key to successful work with young children.

In the penultimate chapter, we turn to New Zealand where Iris Duhn provokes us to consider the view that 'one professionalism does not fit all'. She argues for the notion of professional knowledge-in-the-making and the learning self as a basis for professionalism(s), which she believes requires ongoing engagement with people, things, ideas, policies and politics as part of an ongoing discourse (Dalli and Urban, 2008: 132) and which rejects notions of performativity through measurable outcomes and benchmarks. In the chapter, Duhn describes how one early childhood leader faced challenges to her pedagogy and leadership by participating in a climate of change and risk within her setting, thus embracing a professionalism which involves uncertainty and the unknown. Quoting Arendt, she highlights the importance of a 'space to act', to transform the self in thought and practice (also a theme in Chapter 5). She ends the chapter by highlighting the contribution of professional knowledge in contributing to new understandings of what professionalism(s) in early childhood education may look like if it becomes the continuous process of experiencing and questioning the learning self in its relation to the world.

In the final chapter, we identify what we see as the key themes and issues emerging from the chapters in this book as we look towards a new understanding of what professionalism in the early years means. These include: a professionalism that involves uncertainty and risk taking and that is constantly under the process of reconstruction; a view of professionalism that includes practitioners' views and perspectives and the space in which to reflect and to be reflexive; a consideration of the knowledge base and capabilities required to be and to act professionally; and a re-emergence of an 'ethics of care' and a re-evaluation of the importance of the emotional aspects of working with young children and their families. By 'troubling' the concept of professionalism (see Jayne Osgood, Chapter 8) through books such as this, we can consider what it means to be or to become a professional in the early years.

Final thoughts

The chapters in this book contribute to a critical ecology of early childhood (Dalli, 2007). They lend support to the view that professionalism in the early years is a changing, multi-layered and multi-faceted phenomenon. They provide a valuable addition to the ongoing discourse about the nature of professionalism and professional identities that is about contesting taken-for-granted knowledge and reconstruction of meanings and understandings (Dalli and Urban, 2008). The authors of these chapters raise questions about what it means to be a core worker, leader or manager in complex and changing national and international contexts and they attempt to peel away the layers and challenge traditional conceptions of professionalism and so expose new forms of professionalism for early years work in the 21st century.

Summary

- Professionalism in the early years is something that is constantly under reconstruction.
- Professionalism involves risk taking, uncertainty and the unknown.
- 'An ethics of care', professional knowledge and critical reflection are key to being a professional and acting professionally.
- Professionalism is a multi-layered and multi-faceted concept.

Questions for discussion

1. Identify two questions about your developing professional role that you hope this book will address.
2. What do you think of Moss's view that a professional workforce should be one which includes core workers as professionals (as well as those who are leading or managing provision)?
3. What is the difference between professionalism and being a professional?
4. What do you understand by an 'ethics of care' in relation to working in the early years? *(Higher level question)*

Further reading

Levels 5 and 6

Oberheumer, P. and Scheryer, I. (2008) 'What professional?', *Children in Europe. Aiming High: A Professional Workforce for the Early Years*, 15: 9–12.

In this short article, the authors outline the 'Systems of early education/care and professionalization in Europe' (Seepro) project, which looks at profession-oriented education work in early childhood centres across European countries and considers the type of early childhood professional we might collectively wish for.

Owen, S and Haynes, G. (2010) 'Training and workforce issues in the early years', in *Contemporary Issues in the Early Years* (5th edn). London: Sage.

The chapter offers a useful and concise overview of the background to workforce reform in England and raises issues relating to the roles of the 'new professionals' and leaders.

Levels 6 and 7

Miller, L. (2008) 'Developing professionalism within a regulatory framework in England: challenges and possibilities', *European Early Childhood Education Research Journal*, Special Edition on Professionalism, 16(2): 255–69.

This article provides a critical review of policy developments leading to the creation of the new role of Early Years Professional in England and considers the tensions and challenges of inhabiting such a role within an externally prescribed framework which emphasizes standards and outcomes.

Moss, P. (2008) 'The democratic and reflective professional: rethinking and reforming the early years workforce', in L. Miller and C. Cable (eds) *Professionalism in the Early Years*, London: Hodder/Arnold.

Peter Moss argues for the need for professionalism in the early years but as core workers in the system. He questions how these workers might be understood as professionals and raises questions about the devaluation of early years work and about the market model of early years services.

Websites

www.childrenineurope.org
This website links to the *Children in Europe* magazine which is aimed at all those working with children in the 0–10 age range and provides a forum for the exchange of ideas, information and practice in a European context.

www.cwdcouncil.org.uk
This website provides information, links to policy initiatives, publications and reports relating to early years workforce reform.

References

Abbott, L. and Pugh, G. (1998) *Training to Work in the Early Years.* Buckingham: The Open University Press.

Dahlberg, G. and Moss, P. (2005) *Ethics and Politics in Early Childhood Education*. London and New York: RoutledgeFalmer.

Dalli, C. (2007) 'Towards a critical ecology of the profession', symposium presentation, Annual Conference of the European Early Childhood Education Research Association, Prague, August.

Dalli, C. and Urban, M. (2008) 'Editorial', *European Early Childhood Education Research Journal*, Special Edition on Professionalism, 16(2): 131–3.

Fenech, M. and Sumsion, J. (2007) 'Early childhood teachers and regulation: complicating power relations using a Foucauldian lens', *Contemporary Issues in Early Childhood*, 8(2): 109–22.

Karila, K. (2008) 'A Finnish viewpoint on professionalism in early childhood education', *European Early Childhood Education Research Journal*, 16(2): 210–24.

Members of the British Educational Research Association Special Interest Group (2003) *Early Years Research: Pedagogy, Curriculum and Adult Roles, Training and Professionalism.* Nottingham: British Educational Research Association.

Miller, L. (2008) 'Developing professionalism within a regulatory framework in England: challenges and possibilities', *European Early Childhood Education Research Journal*, Special Edition on Professionalism, 16(2): 255–69.

Miller, L. and Cable, C. (2008) (eds) *Professionalism in the Early Years*. London: Hodder Education.

Miller, L., Dalli, C. and Urban, M. (eds) (forthcoming) *Towards a Critical Ecology of the Profession: Early Childhood Grows Up.* Berlin: Springer Verlag.

Moss, P. (2008) 'The democratic and reflective professional: rethinking and reforming the early years workforce', in L. Miller and C. Cable (eds) *Professionalism in the Early Years*. London: Hodder Education.

Oberheumer, P. (1998) 'A European perspective on early years training', in L. Abbott and G. Pugh (eds) *Training to Work in the Early Years.* Buckingham: The Open University Press.

Oberheumer, P. and Scheryer, I. (2008) 'What professional?', *Children in Europe. Aiming High: A Professional Workforce for the Early Years*, 15: 9–12.

Organisation for Economic Co-operation and Development (OECD) (2006) *Starting Strong II: Early Childhood Education and Care*. Paris: OECD.

Osgood, J. (2006) 'Editorial. Rethinking professionalism in the early years: perspectives from the United Kingdom', *Contemporary Issues in Early Childhood*, 7(1): 1–4.

Simpson, D. (2010) 'Being professional? Conceptualising early years professionalism in England', *European Early Childhood Education Research Journal*, 18(1): 5–14.

Wenger, E. (1998) *Communities of Practice*. Cambridge: Cambridge University Press.

PART 1

LEADING, MANAGING AND NEW PROFESSIONAL IDENTITIES

CHAPTER 2

LEADING AND MANAGING IN THE EARLY YEARS

Mary E. Whalley

Overview

In this chapter, I offer some definitions of 'leadership' and 'management' in an early years context and explore the distinctive and distinguishing features of each. Within the contemporary children's workforce in England, there are two key roles in leadership and management: that of leading and managing an organization and that of leading practice. Often, in small private nurseries and voluntary pre-schools, the roles combine but each is distinctive and it is only relatively recently that concerted attention – either from government or within the academic community – has been given to them. The task of leading and managing integrated children's centres is being supported through the National Professional Qualification for Integrated Centre Leadership (NPQICL) while the role of leader of practice is being developed through pathways to Early Years Professional Status (EYPS). I show how each of these developments is contributing significantly to the 'professionalization' of early years provision and practice. Research consistently 'confirms the crucial role of leadership in creating and sustaining successful and effective organisations' (Leithwood and Levin, 2004, cited in the National College for School Leadership (NCSL), 2007: 4). While the role of the Integrated Centre Leader (ICL) usually combines elements of both leadership

(Continued)

(Continued)

and management, that of EYP is essentially that of leader of practice and does not inherently carry a wider management remit.

A number of key theorists and researchers, including studies from beyond the United Kingdom, have contributed to our current understanding of early years leadership. In particular, I discuss how the European model of 'social pedagogue' has helped shape that of the EYP and suggest a new definition of the 'leader of practice', though I also consider some of the complex issues in training and employment for EYPs. Equally, the challenge of management of integrated centres is noted, with the focus here on multi-professional working. I outline key characteristics of leader and manager, particularly those of supportive and interactive role model and instigator of change. Three case studies are included in the chapter to offer appropriate contextualization of the theoretical aspects being considered.

Defining leadership and management

The terms 'leadership' and 'management' are often used interchangeably – particularly within early years. This is both unhelpful and confusing. Indeed, both these terms are often misunderstood across a range of professional disciplines. Law and Glover (2000, cited in Rodd, 2006) offer helpful insights into the different emphases of the two roles. They encourage an understanding of manager as one who plans and makes decisions, organizes and clarifies work roles, coordinates the organization and generally takes responsibility for monitoring its effectiveness. By contrast, the leader's role is to give direction, offer inspiration, build teamwork, set an example and gain the respect and acceptance of other practitioners. However, it is very difficult to separate leadership from management; indeed, Hall's (1996) study on the role of headteachers shows them to be simultaneously leaders and managers, which led her to the conclusion that 'management without leadership was unethical ... leadership without management irresponsible' (p. 11). Whilst discussion here focuses primarily on the roles of managers/leaders in private, voluntary and independent pre-school settings, I intend that there will also be some relevance for those in positions of leadership in early years provision within maintained schools.

Learning from research

For the past couple of decades, there has been a groundswell of interest in issues relating to leadership and management in the early years. This interest has been global but within the UK since 1997, it has been driven – in part, at least – by the high priority and huge financial investment of the government into raising the quality and status of early years practice and provision (Moss, 2001).

In developing the Effective Leadership and Management Scheme (ELMS-EY), Moyles (2006) draws on several years of research into early years practice (Moyles and